Winsey Caviness

SOUTHERN ABOLITIONIST
WHITE WOMAN

*The amazing story of my great-great grandmother,
a white woman born and raised and residing in the slave state of
North Carolina, fights against slavery therein.*

SIDNEY C. SNEAD

Copyright © 2024 by Mr. Sidney C. Snead
All rights reserved.

Certificate of Registration

This Certificate issued under the seal of the Copyright Office in accordance with title 17, United States Code, attests that registration has been made for the work identified below. The information on this certificate has been made a part of the Copyright Office records.

Maybeth Peters

Register of Copyrights, United States of America

Registration Number:

TX 6-936-796

Effective date of registration:

December 11, 2008

Title ——————————————
Title of Work: Southern Abolitionist White Woman

Completion/ Publication ——————————
Year of Completion: 1998
Date of 1st Publication: May 1, 1998   Nation of 1st Publication: United States

Author ——————————————
Author: Sidney C Snead
Author Created: text, photograph(s), compilation, editing

SIDNEY C. SNEAD
BOOKS

Sidney C. Snead

Dedication

This book is dedicated to my late mother whom I promised to write a book about our family saga.

Contents

Introduction

The amazing story of my great-great grandmother, a white woman born and raised and residing in the slave state of North Carolina, fights against slavery therein.

Winsey Caviness

THE CHILDREN OF WINSEY CAVINESS
Seven Mulatto Offspring By Seven Black Fathers

General Harrison Caviness
Mary Caviness
Winsey Ann Caviness
St. Francis Cavines
Sarah Caviness
Martha Caviness
Hannah Caviness

In the southern regions of the United States, it is commonplace for people to be known by their middle names instead of their first names. The eldest child, General, went by his middle name, Harrison. The third child, Winsey, went by her middle name Ann. The fourth child, St. Francis, went by Francis.

HARRISON

ANN

MARTHA

My great-great grandmother
Winsey Ann Caviness
(white)

Winsey Ann Caviness Maness Shamberger
My great grandmother

My grandfather
Sidney Gaston Maness
(known by middle name Gaston)
Arsia Ritter (wife)

My mother
Hattie John Arah Maness
Merrie Snead (husband)

Myself (my wedding photo)
Sidney C. Snead
SSnead4@aol.com (SSnead4@aol.com)
New Jersey (USA)

I live by the faith that **GOOD** will always triumph over **evil.** No matter what era, there will be people of courage who reaffirm that belief. There will be members of the dominant group who see the evil of their group's actions and have the courage not to be part of it. And courage runs the gamut FROM the elaborate building of a factory by the Nazi member Oskar Schindler in order to protect as many Jews as he could, TO the courage of a Ku Klux Klan member quitting the organization.

I dedicate this webpage to the memory of my great-great grandmother Winsey Caviness, who was one woman of such courage. On behalf of your descendants, and on behalf of all Americans and of all peoples around the world who love freedom: "We are proud of you, we salute you, and we love you Granny Caviness".

OCTOBER 1998

WINSEY (aka Wincy) CAVINESS

My great-great grandmother WINSEY CAVINESS a.k.a. Cavendish, was a white woman born and raised in the antebellum (before the Civil War) slave state of North Carolina ca. 1819. Even though she was a white southerner who lived in a slave society, she was good-hearted and knew even back then that slavery was wrong and wanted to see it abolished. She hated slavery with all her being. An incident that she witnessed was for her the last straw. She saw a slave man being violently mistreated by a white man and it upset her so much that she made this vow: **She would never give birth to a slaveholder! Therefore, she would never have a child by a white man. She would free as many brown babies as she could by giving birth to them, because when the mother was white then the children were born free.**

Slaves were assigned the legal status of property, the same as houses, horses, cows, hogs, barrels of flour, cooking utensils, etc., and could be mortgaged and used for collateral. As such, slaves had an assessed valuation by the taxing authority, and slave owners were assessed property taxes on the value of their slaves along with the other property that they owned. Slaves were assessed a value according to their occupation, age, sex, health, color, intellect, fertility, et al.

Thus, United States had chattel slavery. For example, if you own a female animal and it has offspring, then you own its offspring. However, if a female animal is roaming free (stray), then its offspring are also free. Likewise, slavery in the United States.

In the ante-bellum South, children were born into the status of their mother, regardless of who the father was. If the mother was a slave, then the children were born slaves. If the mother was free, then the children were born free. Winsey was white, therefore free, therefore her children were all born free in ante-bellum North Carolina. Winsey had seven mulatto children, 1 boy, 6 girls: Harrison, Mary, Ann, Frances, Sarah, Martha, Hannah.

(She is listed as white and her children are listed by name as mulatto on the Free schedule in the 1850 and 1860 U.S. Census for Moore County, North Carolina.)

It was illegal to be an abolitionist. She did not have money enough to buy slaves freedom. It was illegal to help slaves escape. Therefore, she took an option available to her to fight for freedom and human dignity.

To settle doubts as to whether a child of an Englishman and a Negro woman should be slave or free:

Virginia Law of 1696 Act. I " Be it enacted that all children born in this country shall be held bond or free only according to the condition of the mother." (Black Laws of Virginia, by June Purcell Guild, LL.M, Whittet & Shepperspn, Reprinted 1969 by Negro Universities Press, a Division of Greenwood Press, Inc. New York, page 25.)

In a case where a woman went to court to gain her freedom from a slaveholder based upon the fact that she was born to a free woman of color, the court ruled in her favor: Slaves N.C. 1858. Where a person was born free, no length of illegal and usurped dominion over him [her] can make him [her] a slave. (Bookfield v. Stanton, 51 NC (Vol. 6 Jones) 156, West's North Carolina Digest, Vol. 35, Signatures to Taxation-818, Beginning 1778, West Publishing Co., St. Paul, MM, Copyright 1991, page 35 NC D 2d-6.)

Article I, Section 9 of the US Constitution forbade the importation of slaves after year 1808. The supporters of this provision hoped that this would put an end to slavery over time. Thus, the purpose of this amendment was defeated by holding the children born to slave mothers as slaves. A master could increase his number of slaves by marrying a slave woman to a desirable slave man or by fathering a slave child himself. More than one of our Presidents were the fathers of mulatto children born to their slave women, according to the oral traditions of their African American descendants, now being confirmed through DNA testing.

President Thomas Jefferson's mulatto son via his liaison with slave Sally Hemings has recently been confirmed through DNA testing.

Linda Allen Bryant says she is a direct descendant of President George Washington and slave Venus through their mulatto son West Ford. Reference, http://www.westfordlegacy.com

Even a Northern President fathered a mulatto child.

My African-American cousin by marriage (now deceased), Marjorie (maiden name?) Caviness (1st) Hughes (2nd) told me that she is a direct descendant of President John Adams.

An example of Winsey's determination to fight slavery was how she endured the **inhumane** oppression of the anti-miscegenation statutes. The anti-miscegenation statutes forbade the commingling of whites and blacks, punishable with heavy penalties of fines and imprisonment against the couple as well as against the minister or justice of the peace:

1. It was illegal for whites and blacks to marry. So although she wanted to be a married mother, she nevertheless had to raise her children as a single parent.

The North Carolina law of 1741 read: For Prevention of that abominable Mixture and spurious issue, which hereafter may increase in this Government, by white Men and women intermarrying with Indians, Negroes, Mustees, or Mulattoes, Be it enacted...That if any white Man or Woman, being free shall intermarry with an Indian, Negro, Mustee or Mulatto man or woman, or any Person of Mixed Blood, to the Third Generation, bond or free, he shall, by Judgment of the County Court, forfeit and pay the sum of Fifty Pounds, Proclamation Money, for the use of the Parish. The law then stated that if any minister or justice of the peace be found guilty of performing a ceremony in violation of the above provisions, he would also have to pay a fine of fifty pounds. The law was re-enacted in 1830 to enjoin the clerk of the county court from issuing a license to a mixed couple, violation of which was punishable by fine and imprisonment. The same penalty was to be meted out to anyone celebrating such a marriage. (Reference Book: The Free Negro in North Carolina 1790-1860, John Hope Franklin, The University of North Carolina Press, Chapel Hill, NC, 1943,1971,1995, pp 36-37.)

2. It was illegal for whites and blacks to live together; this was deemed cohabitation and participants would suffer the same penalties as if they were married. Therefore, she had to raise her children without a father figure in the home.

Miscegenation 45.45 N.C. 1841. The marriage between a free person of color and a white person is null and void, and therefore, when such persons cohabit together, they come within the provisions of the act against adultery and fornication (Rev. St. C 34 Sec. 44) State v Fore, 23 N.C. (Vol. 1 Iredell) 378 (West's North Carolina Digest 2nd, Criminal Law 1-397, Vol. 10, Beginning 1778 covering cases from State and Federal Courts, West Publishing Co., St. Paul, MN. Copyright 1990, page 10 NC D 2d-166.) (This law prevented a mixed couple from going to another state to marry where interracial marriages were legal, and then returning to live as husband and wife in North Carolina.)

3. It was illegal for whites and blacks to live separately but continue to have an ongoing relationship. An ongoing relationship was determined by children—having 1 child out of wedlock would not prove an ongoing relationship because that one child could have been the result of an isolated incident. But having 2 or more children by the same man would be proof of a continuing relationship, and the participants would suffer the same penalties as if they were married. Consequently, she had each child by a different black man in order to protect the fathers and herself from the penalties of the anti-miscegenation statutes. Therefore, she was

precluded from forming a long lasting committed relationship. Each child knew his/her own father.

As legislatures during the slavery era consisted of all white men, these laws requiring a continuing relationship were written by white men for white men. This requirement allowed them to have liaisons with brothel courtesans or independent prostitutes of another race without breaking the miscegenation statutes. As an unintended consequence, Winsey was able to use these same laws to inure to her benefit.

Ark. 1960. Sexual intercourse on one occasion in absence of any indication that parties had lived together otherwise, did not constitute "concubinage" for purposes of statute making it a felony for persons of Caucasian and Negro races to engage in concubinage together. Ark. Stats. Sec. 41806,41-807 Hardin v. State 339, S.W. 2d, 423, 232, Ark. 672 (West's Arkansas Digest Vol. 12A, Master and Servant 203 - Monopolies, West Publishing Co., St. Paul, MN., Copyright 1970, page 12A ARK D-536.)

Ala. App 1930 Evidence merely disclosing single act of intercourse without intention to continue illicit relations was insufficient to establish offense of miscegenation. (Jackson vs. State, 129 So. 306, 23 Ala. App 555. West's Alabama Digest, Vol. 12 beginning 1820, Covenant Action of to Criminal Law 361, West Publishing Co., St. Paul, MN, Copyright 1994, page 12 Ala. 2D-223.)

Many whites were as frustrated over slavery as much as blacks were, and were compelled to deal with their frustrations. John Brown was a white man who dealt with his frustration over slavery by grabbing a gun and taking life. Winsey was a white woman who dealt with her frustration over slavery by giving life.

A white woman who had a white child out of wedlock was often ostracized and had to beg or go into prostitution in order to survive (remember Belle Watling in Gone With The Wind). However, Winsey benefited from the positive effect of the double negative, i.e., if a white woman had black children out of wedlock, people just thought she was upset about something, and left her alone. Therefore, Winsey never had to beg or go into prostitution. There was never anything bad to say about her character.

Winsey was the granddaughter of John Cuit Caviness who fought in the American Revolutionary War. John received mustering out pay at Warrenton, N.C. re: Colonial Records of North Carolina, Halifax County, N.C, XXII, DAR (Daughters of the American Revolution) Guide 64,714. (Reference Book: Henry Cavinis, The Immigrant Infant, and some of his Descendants, Alloa Caviness Anderson, Genealogical Department, Church of Jesus Christ of Latter Day Saints, 1971, call # 929.273 c316a. pp 69-72.) She supported herself by farming the property inherited from him and voluntary child support from each of the fathers. Winsey was a trained midwife and also earned some money this way. None of the children ever passed for white and they all married African-Americans.

Winsey had her first child at about age 23, which was old for a woman to start her family in those days. Her advanced age indicates that she thought long and deeply prior to embarking on her decision. Winsey lived to see her goal of slavery abolished (she died ca. 1900). (Winsey was still young enough to have children after slavery ended—her mother Mariah Caviness had her last child around age 47. The 13th Amendment to the Constitution abolished slavery in 1865. The fact that Winsey did not have more children indicates that the abolishment of slavery was her primary goal.) She always loved her children, her descendants, and the fathers of her children. She has over 900 African-American descendants on her family tree.

Our family never publicized to non family members the fact that we had a white grandmother, because people would automatically know that she wasn't married to any of the fathers (due to the miscegenation statutes) and we would thus be publicizing illegitimacy (although we were happy for what she did). However, I believe that enough historical time has elapsed and the openness of today's society is such that it no longer has to be a family secret.

From my talking to friends and co-workers, I realize that the American public by and large does not know and therefore needs to be aware of the following:

1. Not all blacks in the ante-bellum South were slaves; there was a large number of free blacks.

In the 1860 US Census, there were 3,953,760 slaves; and 488,070 free Negroes in the United States. Of the free colored population, 46.2% was in the North and 44.6% in the South. Therefore, there were almost one-quarter million free blacks in the Southern states prior to the Civil War. Reference: AFRO USA: a reference work on the black experience. Compiled and edited by Harry A. Ploski, Ph.D. (New York University) and Ernest Kaiser (Bibliographer, Schomburg Collection of Negro History and Literature), Published by Bell weather Publishing Co., Inc., NYC, 1971, pages 344-348.

2. Southern white women who gave birth to black babies were not killed (Winsey lived to an old age).
3. Black babies born to Southern white women were not killed nor given away (Winsey's children lived with her to adulthood).
4. Some blacks were born with European names and did not take the name of a slaveholder (freeborn children were born with the name of their mother, white or black.) and therefore do not need to call themselves "X". Many of my cousins who are Winsey's descendants from her son Harrison Caviness still have the French Huguenot surname of Caviness.
5. Mulatto children in the South were also the result of white women and black men, and not solely from white men and black women (the movies "Band of Gold," "Roots," "Queen" and "Sally Hemings" only showed mulatto children resulting from the white man, black woman relationship).

In the slave state of North Carolina, in the case of a white couple, the husband sought a divorce on the grounds that his wife became the mother of a mulatto child. In this case, the plaintiff was denied a divorce because, in marrying her because of pregnancy, he could not presume her to be chaste. Justice Ruffin pointed out that the petitioner was "criminally accessory to his own honor in marrying a woman whom he knew to be lewd." Thus, the husband had to go on acting as the father of this free Negro child.

In another case, a white mother went into court and forced the Negro father of hef child to support their child.

(Reference Book: The Free Negro in North Carolina 1790-1860, John Hope Franklin, The University of North Carolina Press, Chapel Hill, NC, 1943, 1971, 1995, page 38.)

The Delaney sisters state that their great-great grandmother was a white woman named Mrs. Logan living in the slave state of Virginia. A fellow named John Logan, who was white, was an army officer called away to fight during the war of 1812. While he was gone, his wife took up with a Negro slave on their plantation. She was already the mother of seven daughters by her husband, and her romance with the slave produced two more daughters. When the husband returned, he forgave his wife--*forgave her!*-- and adopted the two mulatto girls as his own. They even took his last name, Logan. The two [free] little mulatto girls, Patricia and Eliza, were just part of the family. The only time anyone heard tell of their older, white half sisters mistreating them was when those white girls were old enough to start courting and they used to hide their little, colored half-sisters! They are descended from Eliza Logan. (Reference Book: Having Our Say, The Delaney Sisters' First 100 Years, Sarah L. Delaney and A. Elizabeth Delaney with Amy Hill Hearth, Dell Publishing, New York, NY, 1994, pp. 41-42.)

Ruth Hunt states that her ancestor was a white woman of German heritage named Catherine Cansler who lived in Monroe County, Tennessee prior to the Civil War. She had 3 or 4 free mulatto sons by a favorite slave man whom she purchased, named

Appius. She also had 2 white sons. Reference http://www.tngenweb.org/monroe/3gen.htm

6. Many Southern whites were also against slavery, not only Northern whites.
7. Southern white women with mulatto children were not all isolated, because Winsey lived close by and interacted with her white relatives.
8. Free blacks did not all suffer more than slaves in the South, because Winsey's children all lived to adulthood and married.
9. Slaves were not allowed to marry free blacks.

Slaves. 00 NC 1846. After a free person of color is convicted of marrying a slave before the act of 1845, he cannot be discharged on the ground that the master of the slave consented to the marriage. He should have shown that fact in defense. (State v. Roland, 28 NC 241, American Digest 1656 to 1896, Vol. 44, Shipping to Subscribing Witnesses, West Publishing Co., St. Paul, MN., copyright 1903, page 1043 Sec. 56.)

10. Because a master could free a parent without freeing the children, a black woman could therefore be the parent of slaves and free children in the same household simultaneously, depending upon her status at the time of their birth.

Slaves N.C. 1842. Children born of a slave mother, entitled to or promised her freedom at the end of a fixed period, are born slaves, and so continue even after the mother obtains her freedom. (Mayho v. Sears, 25 NC (Vol. 3 Iredell) 224, West's North Carolina Digest, Vol. 35, Signatures to Taxation-818,

Beginning 1778, West Publishing Co., St. Paul, MN., Copyright 1991, page 35 NC D 2d-6.)

Slaves, VA 1827. When a female slave is emancipated, with a reservation that her future increase shall be slaves, such reservation shall be void, and the woman and her increase are absolutely free. (Fulton v. Shaw, Vol. 4 Rand (25 VA) 597. West's Virginia and West Virginia Digest, Vol. '17, Signatures to Supercedes, 1681 to date, West Publishing Co., St. Paul, MN., Copyright 1968, page 17 Va D-5.)

11. Free blacks had a status similar to today's aliens--they had to have permits to remain in the county/ state.
12. In North Carolina, employers had to teach free blacks how to read, yet it was forbidden to teach slaves to read. (Many agricultural employers couldn't read themselves, so this requirement was often circumvented.)
13. In North Carolina, free blacks had the right to vote, which was later taken away by the legislature.
14. The First Amendment to the US Constitution guarantees the freedom of the press. Yet the slave states were allowed to pass laws making it illegal to publish or disseminate any written word advocating the abolishment of slavery.

Slaves NC 1860 In a prosecution under the statute (Rev. Code C.34,S16), it is not necessary to aver or prove that the **forbidden publication [abolitionist]** was delivered to a slave or free negro [sic], or read in their presence. (Rev. Code, C34, SI6, State v. Worth 52 NC (7 Jones) 488, West's North Carolina Digest Vol. 35. Signatures to Taxation-818, West Publishing

Co., St. Paul, MN, Copyright 1991, page 35NC D2d-16.)

Slaves NC 1860 prohibiting the publication or circulation of any **incendiary [abolitionist]** pamphlet or paper, includes a bound volume, of the tendency named. (Rev. Code, C34, SI 6, State v. Worth 52 NC (7 Jones) 488, West's North Carolina Digest Vol. 35, Signatures to Taxation-818, West Publishing Co., St. Paul, MN, Copyright 1991, page 35NC D2d-16.)

Slaves NC 1860 A book which denounces slavery as worse than theft and as leading to murder, and proclaims that it must be put an end to, even at the cost of blood, certainly has a tendency to excite slaves to insurrection. (Rev. Code, C34, SI6, State v. Worth 52 NC (7 Jones) 488, West's North Carolina Digest Vol. 35, Signatures to Taxation-818, West Publishing Co., St. Paul, MN, Copyright 1991, page 35NC D2d-16.)

15. Many mulatto illegitimate children became landholders via bequests from their white mothers or fathers. (Winsey's son Harrison became one of the first African-American men to own property in Moore County, North Carolina.)
16. President Lincoln wanted to colonize all blacks; the South wanted to colonize only the free blacks. (Why didn't President Lincoln and the South advocate the colonization of all whites back to Europe as they did not believe that we could live together.)
17. The Grandfather clause did not prevent all blacks from voting, because some blacks could prove that their grandfather was white.

18. Why do some whites want to portray a stereotype of black men lusting after white women (ala the movie Birth Of A Nation.) Blacks could look at the life of Winsey and portray a stereotype of white women lusting after black men. Both stereotypes would be inaccurate.

19. Africans entered this country as indentured servants the same as whites prior to slavery. Indentured servants, both black and white, were not slaves but were held for a term of years by contract. Slaves were held for life. Also, some Africans voluntarily immigrated to the colonies as free blacks. As they tended to marry other indentured servants both white and black, other free blacks, Indians (Native Americans), and distant cousins, then there are today African-Americans with no slavery in their American heritage.

During the early period of importation of Negroes into Virginia some of them gained their freedom by proving that they were in fact held by indenture. (Black Laws of Virginia, by June Purcell Guild, LL.M, Whittet & Shepperson, Reprinted 1969 by Negro Universities Press, a Division of Greenwood Press, Inc. New York, Introduction, page 6)

Elsie Taylor Goins family tree leads back to 2 mulatto women who sailed from Africa into Charleston in 1764 as "free people of color." In the 1730's her ancestor William Cleveland, a white European, married the daughter of the African king Skinner Caulker. William's mulatto daughter Elizabeth Cleveland and her niece Catherine sailed from Africa into Charleston in 1764 already free as "free people of color." They later owned slaves and a rice plantation in Berkely

County. Goins has proof that her ancestors arrived as free people in a document signed by the governor and secretary of state declaring that her ancestors from Africa were never held as slaves. Family Traces Roots to Slavery, by Herb Frazier of the Post and Courier, http://www.charleston.net/pub/diaspora/traceroots 0201.htm

Slaves. VA 1859. Though freedom cannot be conferred on a slave except by writing properly recorded, the black's ancestors may always have been free so that he never had any muniment of freedom. (Fulton's Ex'rs v. Gracey, 15 Gratt (56 Va) 314, West's Virginia and West Virginia Digest, Vol. 17, Signatures to Supercedeas, 1681 to date, West Publishing Co., St. Paul, MN., Copyright 1968, page 17 Va D-6.)

20. It was not until 1967 that the US Supreme Court unanimously declared anti - miscegenation statutes unconstitutional.

Proof of my relationship:
  o Winsey A. Caviness, white, single, is the mother of Ann Caviness, mulatto

  o Ann Caviness married Aaron Maness and is the mother of Gaston Maness.

1880 U.S. Census, North Carolina, Moore County, Sheffield Township, page 362, dwelling # 287, family 237 showing 3 generations: Winsey Caviness, mother, white, single/Ann Maness, daughter, mulatto, widow/Gaston Maness, grandson, mulatto.

Gaston Maness married Arsia Ritter and is the father of Hattie Maness Snead.

1910 U.S. Census, North Carolina, Moore County, Sheffield Township, Sheet 4, Family # 66, showing Gaston Maness, father, mulatto/Hattie Maness, daughter, mulatto.

Hattie Maness married Merrie Snead and is my mother (shown on my birth certificate).

The above ancestors are all now deceased.

Genealogy chart:
- *Andre Cabanis - wife?
- *Pierre Cabanis, born 1627 in France, d (?), - wife Anne Soultierre, born 1631 in France

Henri Cabanis - and wife Marie (maiden name unknown) French Huguenots, fled from France, to Switzerland, to England and sailed with infant son Henri (Henry), from Gravesend, England to America on the ship Mary and Ann, George Hawes, Capt., on April 19, 1700 and landed in Virginia on July 31, 1700. (Reference Book: Henry Cavinis, The Immigrant Infant, and some of his Descendants, Alloa Caviness Anderson, Genealogical Department, Church of Jesus Christ of Latter Day Saints, 1971, call # 929.273 c316a.pp 69-72.)
- Henry Cavinis - Jane Allen (wife)
- John Cuit Caviness - Sallie Solomon (wife). John fought in the American Revolutionary War
- Mariah Caviness – single
- Winsey Caviness – single
- Ann Caviness Maness -mulatto - Aaron Maness (husband);(James Shamberger 2nd husband)
- Sidney Gaston Maness - Arsia Ritter (wife)
- Hattie Maness - Merrie Snead (husband)
- Sidney C. Snead

*An asterisk marks individuals who are still in question.

NOVEMBER 1998

BALLAD OF LORD THOMAS (Author Unknown)

[A historical song of the old South, retold from Arsia Ritter Maness (my grandmother) to her children Ollie Maness Pope (my aunt) and Hattie Maness Snead (my mother)]

Sometime after the Civil War before the turn of the century (1900's) in the state of North Carolina in the days of official segregation, there occurred a true story of the love of a white man for a black woman. The white man was a person of very high status in the community such as a commissioner or alderman, but the anti-miscegenation statutes forbade the intermarrying of whites and blacks. (Thankfully, marriages between whites and blacks are now legal throughout our country.) Like Romeo and Juliet, this beautiful love ended in tragedy. Unlike Romeo and Juliet, this was not written by Shakespeare; this really happened. The story appeared in the local press. But in those days many persons could not read nor write. The news of the day was often made into a song and spread through the town this way. In the original song, Lu Ellen was also called Fair Ellen and the brown girl did not have a name. (I asked my mother if the brown girl was a relative of ours and she said she didn't know; it's significant that she didn't say no.) Because the US Census did not list slaves by name, I took the liberty to give the brown girl the name Thala Mae (fictitious) out of respect. There are more stanzas but these are all that they could remember. The song is sung in the slow, soulful tradition of black spirituals. Be still, and let your mind drift back to the wistful time of a bygone era in American history.

Lord Thomas was a white man
A very fine man was he
He was the lord of many fine things
And held a strong post in the community

Lu Ellen was a white girl
And she loved Lord Thomas well
But Lord Thomas loved Thala Mae
And with her he wanted to dwell

Now Thala Mae was a black girl
She was beautiful and brown
And Lu Ellen was a fair skinned girl
Whose beauty was renown

Lord Thomas loved Thala Mae
And wanted to marry her
But his parents objected with such a fuss
And caused a great big stir

You can't marry Thala Mae, they said
She is beautiful, but brown
And you know that white folks can't marry Negroes
According to the laws in this town

Thala Mae is a wholesome girl they said
On that no one can dispute
But if you many a black girl
You become a white man of ill repute

We advise you to marry Lu Ellen
Take her for your bride
She is a very fair skinned girl
Who would make any man burst with pride

Lord Thomas said Lu Ellen is fair
On that I agree with you
But her heart is full of deceit

And that I know to be true

I know that the laws forbid white and black to marry
Said Lord Thomas with command
But such laws are an abomination to God
And such laws should be banned

If I can't marry Thala Mae he said
Then we shall live the same as man and wife
For there is none more willing than us
To live without causing any strife

So Lord Thomas and Thala Mae united
And there could never be
A man and woman more perfect to live
In Peace, Love, and Harmony

When Lu Ellen heard about their uniting
She went into a rage and was fit to be tied
Lord Thomas has to marry me, she said
I must be his bride

She sat right down and wrote to Lord Thomas
That she must see him soon
For she was very troublesome about him
And didn't know what to do

The day arrived for the appointed time
And Lu Ellen asked a girlfriend to take a ride
For she could not call on a man alone
In order to keep her pride

Lu Ellen was dressed to impress
And had put on her silk so fine
She topped it off with a dazzling ring
As ever the sun did shine

They rode till they came to Lord Thomas' house
And Lu Ellen knocked on the door

Lord Thomas answered politely
And escorted them across the floor

Come in, come in, Lord Thomas said
Sit right down inside
I'd like you to meet Thala Mae
My lovely, lovely bride

Is this your bride Lu Ellen said
1 tell you, she's monstrous brown
You could have married a fair skinned girl
The fairest girl in town

Lu Ellen had a penknife
With no hesitation before her start
She drew it from her bosom
And pierced Thala Mae in her heart

Lord Thomas said
What's going on? Why do you look so pale?
You used to have the fairest skin
As was ever put under a veil

O darling
Don't you see what's the matter with me?
For Lu Ellen has caused my own heart's blood
To come trickling down to my knees

Lord Thomas took his sword
He swung
And cut off Lu Ellen's head
And threw it against the wall!!

Lord Thomas went to Thala Mae
And saw his dying bride
He then lay his body against the upturned sword
And pierced his own insides

Lu Ellen's friend
Who was standing horrified at bay
Heard Lord Thomas' final words
As he passed away

"Go *bury my, go bury me*
Dig my grave so deep
Go bury Thala Me in my arms
But Lu Ellen under my feet, my feet

Lu Ellen under my feet."

ADDENDUM

Towards the end of Frederick Douglass'
life, a young man asked him "What must
we do to continue the struggle?"
Frederick Douglass answered "Agitate!"
"Agitate!" "Agitate!"

The bus I rode

Saturday, August 24, 2013. Some of the many buses at a rest stop, on their way to the 50th Anniversary of The March on Washington, D.C.

August 24, 2013

Myself participating in the 50th Anniversary of the
March on Washington

August 24, 2013 Washington, D.C.
Myself with Attorney General Eric Holder on the
big screen

August 24, 2013
Myself in front of the Lincoln Monument

August 24, 2013 Washington, D.C.
Myself with Washington Monument
in the background

August 24, 2013 Washington, D.C.
Myself with the Jefferson Memorial
in the background.

August 24, 2013 Washington, D.C.
Myself in front of the Vietnam Memorial

August 24, 2013 Washington, D.C.Myself in front of the Vietnam Memorial Wall

August 24, 2013 Washington,
D.C. Myself in front of the Dr. Martin
Luther King, Jr. Memorial

August 24, 2013 Washington, D.C.

"I have the audacity to believe that peoples everywhere can have three meals a day for their bodies, education and culture for their minds, and dignity, equality, and freedom for their spirits."
Dr. Martin Luther King, Jr. Memorial quote

SOUTHERN ABOLITIONIST
WHITE WOMAN

Children born of a slave mother, entitled to or promised her freedom at the end of a fixed period, are born slaves, and so continue even after the mother obtains her freedom.

When a female slave is emancipated, with a reservation that her future increase shall be slaves, such reservation shall be void, and the woman and her increase are absolutely free.

Sidney C. Snead has a M.S.W. from Rutgers Graduate School of Social Work. He participated in the August 28, 1963 march on Washington to hear Dr. Martin Luther King, Jr give his "I Have A Dream" speech. He also participated in the 50th anniversary of that historic event in D.C. on August 24, 2013. He is a Vietnam War veteran. Sidney's favorite hobby is genealogy, and he can trace his family back 10 generations.

9 798330 430543